MAKING TENS
Groups of Gollywomples

Based on the Math Monsters™ public television series, developed in cooperation with the National Council of Teachers of Mathematics (NCTM).

by John Burstein

Reading consultant: Susan Nations, M.Ed., author/literacy coach/consultant

Math curriculum consultants: Marti Wolfe, M.Ed., teacher/presenter; Kristi Hardi-Gilson, B.A., teacher/presenter

WEEKLY (WR) READER®
EARLY LEARNING LIBRARY

Please visit our web site at: **www.earlyliteracy.cc**
For a free color catalog describing **Weekly Reader® Early Learning Library's** list
of high-quality books, call 1-877-445-5824 (USA) or 1-800-387-3178 (Canada).
Weekly Reader® Early Learning Library's fax: (414) 336-0164.

Library of Congress Cataloging-in-Publication Data

Burstein, John.
    Making tens: groups of gollywomples / by John Burstein.
       p. cm. — (Math monsters)
    Summary: As they fill holiday gift boxes with different colored gollywomples for their
ten friends, the four monsters learn about grouping numbers when counting and adding.
    ISBN 0-8368-3812-2 (lib. bdg.)
    ISBN 0-8368-3827-0 (softcover)
    1. Counting—Juvenile literature. 2. Addition—Juvenile literature. [1. Counting.
2. Addition.] I. Title.
QA113.B8875   2003
513.2'11—dc21
                                                 2003045042

This edition first published in 2004 by
Weekly Reader® Early Learning Library
330 West Olive Street, Suite 100
Milwaukee, WI 53212 USA

Original Math Monsters™ animation: Destiny Images
Art direction, cover design, and page layout: Tammy Gruenewald
Editor: JoAnn Early Macken

Printed in the United States of America

1 2 3 4 5 6 7 8 9 07 06 05 04 03

You can enrich children's mathematical experience by working with
them as they tackle the Corner Questions in this book. Create
a special notebook for recording their mathematical ideas.

Number Concept and Math

It's important for children to understand that in math, there can be
many ways to arrive at the same answer. They gain an understanding
of this principle by exploring the combinations that equal ten.

Meet the Math Monsters™

ADDISON

Addison thinks
math is fun.
"I solve problems
one by one."

Mina flies
from here to there.
"I look for answers
everywhere."

MINA

MULTIPLEX

Multiplex
sure loves to laugh.
"Both my heads
have fun with math."

Split is friendly
as can be.
"If you need help,
then count on me."

SPLIT

We're glad you want to take a look
at the story in our book.

We know that as you read, you'll see
just how helpful math can be.

Let's get started. Jump right in!
Turn the page, and let's begin!

It was holiday time in Monster Land. The Math
Monsters were thinking of gifts to give. They sang
a holiday song.

"Holiday time with holiday cheer
is the very best time of year.
Joyful days are almost here.
We love holiday time."

"What would our friends like?" asked Multiplex.

"Cookies?" asked Split.

"We gave cookies last year," said Addison. "Let's give them something else."

What kind of gifts do you like to give?

Mina asked, "How about fruit? Our friends really like fruit."

"What kind?" asked Multiplex.

"Let's go ask Aunt Two Lips. She has lots of fruit in her garden shop," said Mina. "I am sure she will help us."

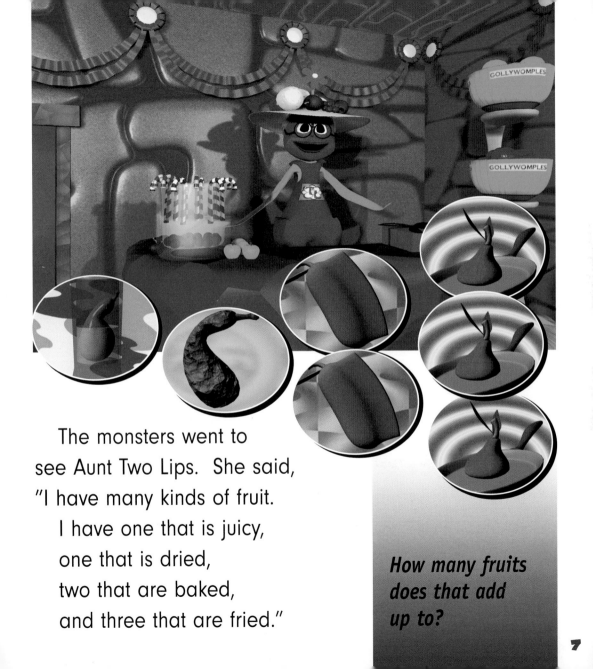

The monsters went to
see Aunt Two Lips. She said,
"I have many kinds of fruit.
I have one that is juicy,
one that is dried,
two that are baked,
and three that are fried."

How many fruits does that add up to?

Ivan Idea
Dextris Digit
Noah Number
Ima Fraction
Clara Fy
Dee Vide
Uncle Z Row
Mae Trix
Ann Sir
Mat O'matics

"You have seven kinds of fruit," said Split.

"Do you have any gollywomples?" asked Addison.

Aunt Two Lips said, "I have lots and lots of gollywomples — blue ones and green ones."

"Great," said the monsters. "All ten friends on our list love gollywomples."

Aunt Two Lips showed the monsters a pile of gift boxes.

"You can put ten gollywomples in each box," she said.

If they give ten gollywomples to each of their ten friends, how many do they need?

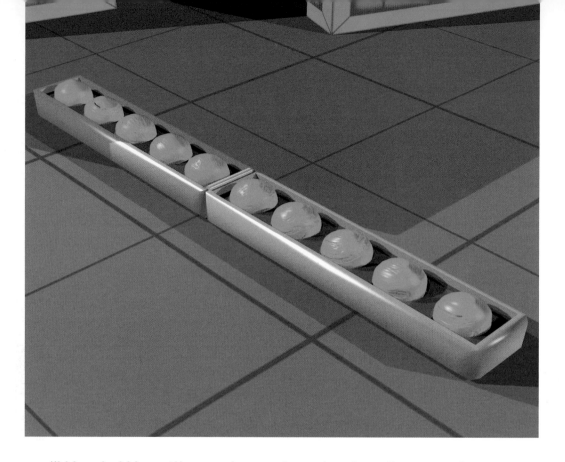

"Wow! We will need one hundred gollywomples in all," said Addison.

"Uncle Z Row likes green," said Mina. "Let's fill one box with ten green gollywomples."

"Cousin Clara likes green, too,
but not as much," said Mina.
"Let's give her a box with nine
green gollywomples and one blue."
"How many does that make?"
asked Addison.

How many do
you think?

"Nine and one make ten," said Multiplex with a smile. "We can give her nine greens and one blue."

"We made a box of ten with nine green gollywomples and one blue," said Addison. "Can we make a box of ten with one green gollywomple and nine blue ones?"

What do you think?

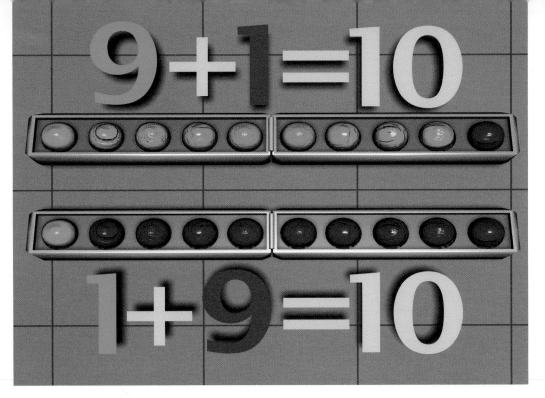

The monsters filled a new box. They put in one green gollywomple and nine blue ones.

"Wow! One and nine also make ten," said Mina.

The monsters sang a little song.

"Nine and one,

one and nine —

for making ten,

they both work fine."

"Let's make a box with eight greens," said Split.

"How many blues do we need?" asked Multiplex.

If the monsters use eight greens, how many blues do they need to make ten?

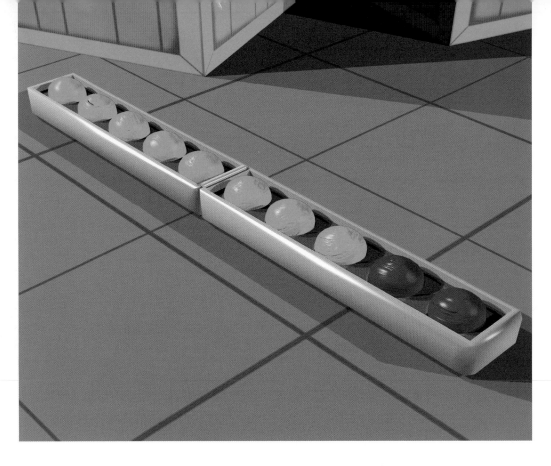

"We need two blues," said Mina. "Eight and
two make ten."

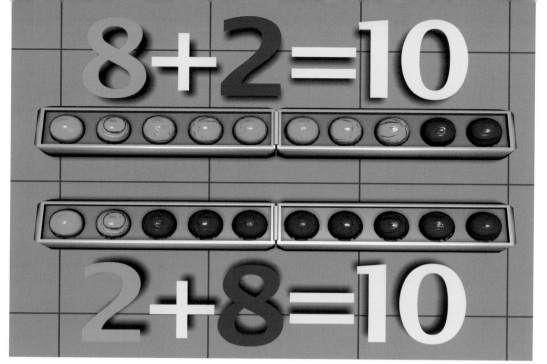

"Two and eight also make ten," said Addison.

The monsters sang a little song.

"Eight and two,
two and eight —
for making ten,
they both work great."

"Are there any other ways we can make ten?" asked Mina.

Can you think of any other ways to make ten?

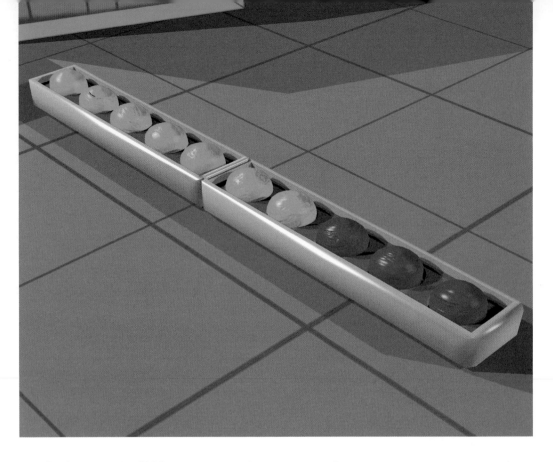

Split said, "We can make ten with seven greens and three blues."

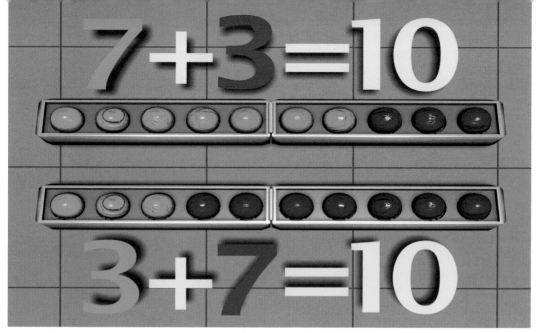

"Seven and three make ten," said Addison.
"So do three and seven."

The monsters sang a little song.

"Three and seven,
seven and three —
both make ten,
as you can see."

"Let's try one more," said
Multiplex. "I think I can make
a box of ten in a new way."

*What do you think
Multiplex will try?*

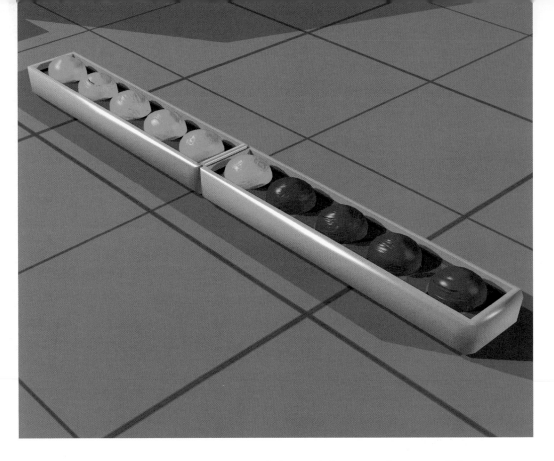

"I can use six greens and four blues. Six and four make ten," said Multiplex.

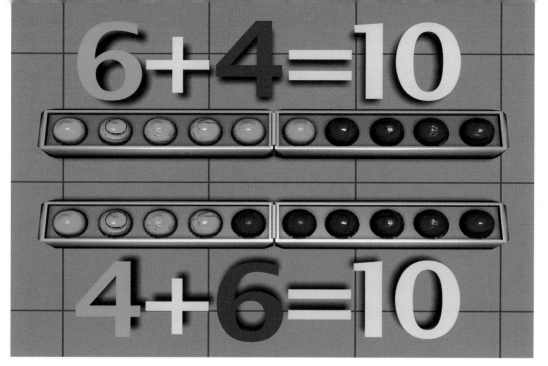

"So do four and six," said Mina. "This is fun!"

The monsters sang a little song.

"Four and six,

six and four

make ten and never

less or more."

"Are there any more ways to make ten?" asked Split. "Are we all done?"

What would you tell Split?

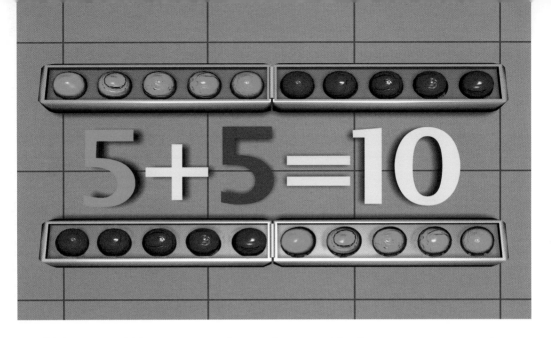

"I know. We can make a box with five greens and five blues," said Addison. "Five and five make ten."

The monsters sang a little song.

"On five and five
you can depend
to always make
the number ten."

"Is that all we can do?" asked Multiplex.

"Let's line up all our boxes," said Mina. "Maybe we can see other ways to make ten."

The monsters put all the boxes in order.

"I see a pattern," said Mina. "Do you?"

"Yes," said Addison. "From the top, each box has one less green and one more blue."

"From the bottom, each box has one more green and one less blue," said Split.

"They all add up to ten," said Multiplex. "Ten boxes for ten friends."

How many ways did the monsters find to make ten? Can you see one more way?

ACTIVITIES

Page 5 The Math Monsters' situation can provide an introduction to a discussion about the importance of giving at holiday time.

Page 7 You might want to lay out materials children can use to count. This is also an opportunity to integrate art with math. For example, children can draw fruit or cut out pictures from a magazine.

Page 9 Have fun counting by tens. Help children build their own gollywomple boxes out of egg cartons by using ten of the egg compartments. You can use them to work through other problems.

Pages 11, 13, 15, 17, 19, 21 Simulate the monsters' problems with the children. Explore ways to make ten using your homemade gollywomples and gollywomple boxes. You can use use green and purple grapes to represent gollywomples or make gollywomples out of green and blue clay. You might even use colored eggs.

Page 23 Encourage children to make predictions by drawing gollywomple boxes in order and then filling them in. Have children record all the ways they can use their egg cartons to make tens.